in case of emergency press

We are proud to acknowledge the Traditional Owners of country throughout Australia and to recognise their continuing connection to land, waters, and culture. We pay our respects to their Elders.

We support recognition, reconciliation, and reparation.

Which way is that thing I don't like?

Nick Crowley

in case of emergency press
https://icoe.com.au
Travancore, Victoria
Australia

Published by in case of emergency press 2025

Copyright © Nick Crowley 2025
All rights reserved. Without limiting the rights under copyright reserved above, no part of this publication may be reproduced, stored in or introduced into a database and retrieval system or transmitted in any form or any means (electronic, mechanical, photocopying, recording or otherwise) without the prior written permission of both the owner of copyright and the above publishers.

ISBN: 978-0-6486111-8-9

Cover Drawing: **Don Clemente**
Homage to Picasso and Dali c. 2021
Ink Pen on Paper

Acknowledgements

I'd like to thank Valentina Udovičić for her ongoing support, and for her shrewd and unsparing feedback on my poems. I'd like to thank Paul Burns for their valuable suggestions on the first draft of this collection.

Dedication

Dear Val,

Stick to the plan.

Table of Contents

fun I	1
fun II	2
challenge painter	3
high	4
nicotine	6
the proceed	7
morning	8
bad memory	9
san jose	10
Lana	11
juice	12
contempt	13
monster	14
manboob	15
nude	16
cake	17
defeat	18
central	19
mexican side	20
I think my new friend is becoming my therapist	21
I think my friend is becoming my lover	22
10 minute coffee high	24
kissing a grandpa	25
another love poem	26
the things we can do	27
timely	28
agave	30
listen to your body?	31
panic	32
astro girl	33
whats the gasometer?	34
rest	35

girlfriend	36
take some time	37
trust	38
big wound	39
continued	40
rest again	41
Boca Sea God	42
I think i'm becoming my own therapist	43
I ate eggs	44
Little Donkey Boy	45
latex chief	46
which way is that thing I don't like	47
Everytime I stop I start again	49
you can do things that never happened	51
i'm allowed to leave reality if i want to	52
About the Author	55

Which way is that thing I don't like?

Nick Crowley

fun I

Having fun isn't that fun
 when you start speaking, the room begins to shrink
  when you look at a face, with a headache, lie compulsively,
   something about the food being shit at a restaurant you've
   never been to
    your chest hurts
     but the cardiologist said there was nothing wrong
      and when you go home early, you stay up, alone,
       till sunrise
        what's that about?

But ok, sometimes when you look good and you're out and
about and you stole your housemate's dexies; people like you.
  Moments of fracture
   where you fumble about with a flick of spirit
    and say something something insipid;

     "this is all absurd"
      "i'm learning all the time"

       and then the crack slips sideways, crushing waves of
       something-just-off-comfort;
       boredom, substance, flat, familiar
        people are talking about television
         and here comes the familiar cocktail of guilt and
         contempt

And I suppose that whole rigmarole is kinda cool

Although I wouldn't call it fun

fun II

I want to write a book about having fun
 I think I'd call it

  'The way things should work'

Here's the problem though
 i'm not a bridge, i'm a spiral
  which models different versions of itself to itself,
   wondering which one you'd like the best

   let's talk quick for a couple minutes
    my heart's about to seal
     i'll say i need to pee
      but really, is it just more comfortable
       to be uncomfortable alone?

   So I consider myself unqualified to write that book
    i'd rather talk theory in wizened circles
     with people who know they know how to have fun
      but aren't quite sure if they've ever had any

challenge painter

Having fun is a stick of needles and guilt
 prodding you around the city
  catch an uber 'cause you're running late
   miss the best part of the night
    where you're alone on the tram with your headphones in

You're only nice if you're literally hanging from the walls
 with good vibes and a good take
  etiquette dictates that the people you feel sad around
   are the people you hate

 please listen actively
  ask good questions
   and if you smoke weed and spend the whole night staring
   at the table cloth
    well that's fine as long you're still a 'funny cunt'

Did you know that my colleague once rated my sense of humour out of ten?

Apparently I'm a 6.5

 So best not be tired
  and picking the elastic bits out of my socks
   and thinking about how big the harpoons must be on
   whaling boats

you're sinking in the cool black ocean with a fisherman sandwiched onto you like a

 burger topping, the harpoon functions well as a tooth pick

  this cold harpoon-tooth-pick-burger is a picture someone
  should paint

   let's say it's this intertextual art event that kept me afloat

high

People inevitably tell me about
 well
  acid and mushrooms

I get it
 you glimpsed the divine pulse of adventure
  tell me about your algorithm shame
   Alan Watts and Terrence McKenna and cloudy ethereal music
    and now you're uneasy and bringing the mystery into every
    damn potluck
     unfortunately catching it is killing it
      like the impotence of a tongue trying to taste itself
       do i really believe that mysticism amounts to quietism
       or is it just that i can't be bothered killing my ego?

   But why not take drugs?
    let's spend our whole lives unhappy
     but content that for moments here and there,
      we were really onto something
       before we woke up on the flats
        joints locked with the inevitable world

Let's pay homage to the dirty evenings
 invoke the jelly, the continuous possibilities
  where freedom makes anything happen
   as long as it commits to making something happen

    Ok but what I'm actually doing
     is calling Paul
      trying to figure out whether I'm having a heart attack
       or a panic attack

Tomorrow morning I'll say it's time to take a break
 but tomorrow night I'll know
  'that was just my inner atheist talking and fuck that shit'
   and if you tell me
    that life can be alive without its painful extremes
     i will argue about the merits of feeling sad
      in a way that probably seems a little neurotic

nicotine

It's fun to swim about the faces in the crowd
　some of us lock eyes
　　yep, we're both scared

It's also fun to look down at your phone
　and walk in a straight line
　　Bodies fall past you
　　　like the contours of a rain drop around a hard wing

But now I've got my pants down in the furthest cubicle
　letting myself slowly drip
　　as I take swills of nicotine spray and spit it between my legs

You see,
　once you're past security
　　being high at the airport is actually pretty fun

the proceed

You have never felt the full force of modernity
 until you've tried to write a poem on Microsoft word
  and found out that something that can only be described as
   psychedelic dad rock
    really 'gets' my emotional landscape.

I got high
 but first I asked my sister if she was ok with me lighting up on her balcony
  props to the bots that made the latest fad 'talking about boundaries'
   what a relief, the world spirit finally confessed
    we never knew how to care
     how to love
      you're not a monster dummy
       you're a student

morning

All the horrible things i've ever done
 i keep them in a chest
  which explodes 1-2 times a week
   this is the closest thing i know to disaster

On the tram, no one speaks
 is everyone sad, or is that just me?
  i imagine mexico city
   i bet people talk there

Modernity is having four minutes to write a poem
 and feeling good about it because it made you
  "pump it out"

bad memory

Well in a way I'm just procrastinating
  but then again
    about half an hour ago
      i sensed one of those little bursts of speed across my torso
        that i can only describe as a message from god
          i don't remember what she said

There is something important on my screen
  that i dare not look in the eye
    it's got to do with me
      and all the things i don't like about myself
        i'm trying to write a novel

Someone told me once,
  'look at it in the light'
    but they don't know that one time
      i saw a dying bug on a lamp

But lamps are not an inspired topic
  and as I said
    about half an hour ago
      i was really onto something

It was just before I was kicking a tarty soccer ball
  around my sister's living room,
    dazed out looping a chain of regrettable thoughts
      i thought I heard her coming home
        so I leaped onto the couch
          opened my book
            and pretended to read.

san jose

My feet sweat beneath a waxy old blanket
  the mountains, the clouds come close
   and stuff up the space between objects
    and when i lift up my blanket i get a blast of BO
     and to be honest
      i kinda like the smell

Which way is that thing I don't like?

Lana

I have a friend called John
 he sleeps in my room
  we're not talking
   we have nothing to say

Another thing, I've finally had my Lana moment
 the last thing i told John is that i finally get it
  i even have a niche favourite song;
   Sweet Carolina from Blue Bannisters

I take little pockets of solitude filled with music
 where i feel clear, empty
  i'd almost call it peace
   except i'm kind of bored

It's hard to have fun alone
 when all you're thinking about
  is whether other people would think that what you're doing is cool.
   there is pleasure, sometimes, all hot and toxic and tinged with disgust
    maybe you 'get' the tragedy of swag becoming ironic
     maybe someone laughed at something you said
      maybe you score a surprised and welcoming smile
       because you didn't seem like the Lana type

juice

I find it difficult to go to bed
  days are to be juiced
    when the organism tries to close
     it looks around for crumbs
       late scraps of time could yield a shot of worth

     i'm not looking very hard
       Instagram is a comfortable living room
         the locus of creature comforts for us mental ones
        our feet are up
          and we're resting our souls to the limit of decay

        Going to sleep is like putting your bed outside
        those terrible minutes where you finally face
              yourself
         before you drift to teeth-ground dreams you won't
         remember

Which way is that thing I don't like?

contempt

Take a seat at a tourist café
 to my glee the guy at the bar
  never misses a beat;
   if you really study the fundamentals
    Bitcoin can work for you

He confesses that owning stuff
 has never gone well
  better to keep your tokens
   in the strongest computing system in the world
   it's never been hacked

But let's not get ideological about it
 in the financial decentralization community
  they say do your own research
   but they also say there is a war going on against the centralists

They'll get one more beer
  drink it speaking Spanish
   the older guy takes the floor
    talks about variegated
    and unremitting
     back problems
      the doctors who insist on prescribing him covid
       woke culture and
        women who won't take a joke

monster

Fifty meters out
 a man flails about
  bad at butterfly in the remnant light of the day

At dusk the sharks come closer to shore
  i keep an eye out

Until i get bored
 and earnest concern fades to lusty hope
  i pray for a black fin

I'd run to the shore, yell mutely to the wind
  left hoarse and realising there's nothing to do but watch
   i'd feel holy

    The mesmerizing death rattle
     faint screams on the wind
      his limbs slash the water
        the gleaming flashes of black leather

A little explosion of hot white water
  then the sea falls calm and amnesic

   He finishes a lap
    i'm berating myself

Which way is that thing I don't like?

manboob

I'm shy to be shirtless in front of other people
 i have what they call
   man boobs

They look better when my nipples are taut
 i compulsively twist them
   call it damage control

But these days are hot and humid
 growing up means putting your needs first
   so i walk bravely through the street
    flaunting them for all they're worth

nude

At the nudist beach
 trying not to seem like a perve
  i haven't seen many naked bodies before

I find it fascinating
 but not in a creepy way

All this air and sunlight
 must be good for my genital health
  my modest package
   lives in dark damp cotton caves
    lined with sweat and remnant piss

It's easy to get lost in old fantasies
 not the one where I bed an older man
  that was kinda traumatic
   the one where people like me
    and spark up spontaneous conversations
     because they think i'm interesting
      or that my body looks good
       lightly sweating
        in the midday sun

cake

They're selling slices of carrot cake
  under an orange sky

For the last time
 let me tell you what i'm thinking;
  all these hours plumbing my depths with that
    suffocating mixture of depression and ego and ash
     going in circles
      wondering when everyone will 'get me'
       but watch the free flow of the earth
        watch it snake and convulse and strike up
         little crystals of beauty and myth
         like the lovely meniscus
           that forms between one thing small and one thing poetic
            its probably geometrical, but all together
            photogenic, but not too tumblr

So, a man walks down the beach
 wearing nothing but a fanny pack
  half covering his cock

They approach him with a naked slice of cake
'no thanks'
 not even a thickening deal can break the fast;
  'they've got weed in em'
   another no
    another neurotic giggle
     it's nice to know that everyone is just as uncomfortable as me

defeat

Ruby is the coolest bitch ever
 she told me to say that in a room
  where shadows move to the rhythm of candlelight
   the one where she's sitting on the couch
    and trying to talk us out of the spooky drug vibe

Predictably enough,
 Paul is in the kitchen spruiking gozleme
  wanting us to want the things they want

Ruby is looking through sheets of music
 she hasn't done this in ages
  the one where she starts and stops and
   finally says yes, Paul
    i'll have some of your gozleme
     somehow this feels like a personal defeat

But don't get too big for your boots... Paul
 i don't want the things that you want
  i'm moving out of my renouncing agency phase

Ruby is saying that she can't fucking play it
 but the plates are in the kitchen drawer
  and she's taking half of what Paul's hawking

central

I just bought a vape
 my sister says it's better than smoking

I've been in a deep and obsessive depression
 because i want to be famous
  (well actually, I'm traumatised but at the time of writing I
  hadn't figured that out)
    the communal need inverted
     a sick modern idiom
      i dislike almost everyone i meet
      the others spell doom
        because i'm probably falling in love with them
         i think i read that on Instagram, but i'll claim it

mexican side

She doesn't want to write a poem
 so there go my dreams of having an edgy writer gf
  she feels foggy, TV tired
   she could write a poem about that

Her skin is burnt from roof tops
 between walls people speak like they're upset
  and i have no idea what they're saying
   and as long as no one gets violent
    i don't really care
     i used to be shocked when people hurt each other

I've been getting into all this 'healing' business that's going around
 we took mushrooms
  talked about how we really felt
   we did a breath work ceremony
    found a bank of traumatic memories
     we're healing, at least on paper
      although she's beginning to suspect
       that i'm the darkness in her life

I'm trying
 to not compulsively listen to songs that i fell in love with when
 i was sixteen
  letting go of old feelings
   which burn my hand to hold
    she says i've come a long way
     and i agree because if that's not true
      then maybe we can't be friends
       trust me, i'm team healing
        but i still have unhealed urges

I think my new friend is becoming my therapist

She tells me in no uncertain terms
  that anxiety is just adrenaline
   which with a little alchemy
    could be turned into magic

I have a friend now
 she believes i've closed a chapter
  she thinks a revolution is happening in the new generation
   the ones who get curious about their sensations
    the ones who exalt their anger
     the ones who smell the old age in their pain
      the ones who smell the trauma in achievement
     the ones who know love is not chemistry
      and soothing is not joy
       i know a healer

It's okay to be sad
 but she thinks its unbecoming
  the way i blatantly externalise it
   and whine about situations
    which i've chosen to put myself in

She said that i was safe to create
 so why am i warding off a panic attack
  by compulsively skipping songs
   she can be my superego now
    she says i can parry the shadows with a good mantra
     and trust the art that i love

I think my friend is becoming my lover

We spent the day together, sitting on the terrace
  i showed you an earlier poem
    the one about therapy

In the evening we stopped talking
 we stared at each other
  i watched you growing old
   with pain leaking from your face

You googled forums about spirit bonds
 we walked along the edge of confession

You said my jumper looked soft
  i asked if i could sit next to you
   our bones knocked

My chest ached until it didn't
 it became an ocean
  where little satellites float around
   on bubbles of light

I said i wasn't scared of you
 i was just scared i would hurt you
  you laughed
   i sounded like a fuckboy

i told you not to worry
 my heart tore wide open
  my chest became an ocean
   that wanted to hold your pain
    but then i was like
     do i have a saviour complex?

Which way is that thing I don't like?

Afterwards we found it difficult to talk
 no one would say what it all meant
  inside i cried "Love!"
   i'm falling in love

Today i woke up with a tight chest
 the ocean had become a pincer dry web
  i can pump out abandonment fantasies at a rate of knots
   in the pockets of quiet i convince myself i could marry her

Tonight we'll stay up till dawn
 and spend all morning in the sheets
  i've fallen in love before

In the early morning
 we go out and smoke cigarettes
  you were dissolving into white light
   i almost cried

I left in the afternoon
 i've decided to get my own place, i had some inspections
  i want a little flat with a garden
   i want to keep a spare toothbrush in the bathroom
   i want you to stay over whenever you want

In the evening i listen to resilient indie rock songs
 and try to find myself again
  was it cringe when i told you
     that i finally get what it means to swim in someone's eyes?

10 minute coffee high

I thought for a moment that i was a god
 i thought that everything would be ok
  from now till death
    the whole world would be a playground
     i enjoyed every dish i washed

Which way is that thing I don't like?

kissing a grandpa

Her hair felt like wire,
 the room was oversaturated
  yet things still fell into place
   but only for like two seconds
    but at least at some point in time
     someone knew something

I'm sorry i never got your eye drops
 i love the way you put them in so fearlessly
   i'm trying to convince you that i'm a good dancer
    (she's never seen me dance)

You accuse me of losing your things
 your gum, your vape
  you accuse me of writing poems about you
   the other day i showed you one
    that very night we fell in love
     so i can't tell whether i'm happy in love
      or happy my writing made you fall in love
       let the record show that I warned her from the beginning
       that i had narcissistic tendencies

You know we can cuddle
 without it turning into sexy time
  you say 'sexy time'
   makes you think of kissing a grandpa

Your mind is reversing back
 and skipping forward
  and driving around the block
   and stopping by
    just to say hi.

another love poem

She doesn't like sharing food from her plate
 but she gave me a slice of her pancake
  love changes people
   opens chests, erodes integrity

She talks sometimes about her 'broski ex'
 but these are very different times
  where every night
   you hang out with a foreign person
    in a foreign country
     and get her to smoke weed for the first time in ten years

She journals with coloured textas
 i journal in all black
  she keeps saying that i'm the darkness in her life
   but upon reflection
    that's not such a bad thing

She's got a fake UE Boom, a penchant for punk
 and a fine line
  between meditating and falling asleep
   and quick hands, raising her head from the pillow
    to scribble down downloads from her spirit guides
     received in a delicate phantasia

Which way is that thing I don't like?

the things we can do

We can turn to water
 we can let the little tremors
  the little tensions in our temples
   fall away
    walking on yellow streets
     sleeping in pink sheets
      go back to headaches
       go again and pump all the energy in fantasy
        you're shortening the loop
         each time you come back to that cool calm that soothes
         it all out

We can follow body highways
 where our souls are the intelligence of traffic
  having bumps and bursts of speed

We can have romance
 we can wonder
  we can have fun for the first time in a long time
   sitting in cool air, waiting the morning out to watch it grow humid
    or maybe we'll lie and doom scroll for hours
     and then shame spiral because we could have been writing
      romanticised accounts of getting breakfast in the city
       soaking up our youth

timely

'Wawa by the Ocean' is a spectacular song
  with harps
    and pitch shifts
      and delay pedals
        that melt the heart of the sound

Other songs have flutes
 and patter in rhythms
  which awaken adventure
    something about a heart seeing a sunrise

When I listen to the murmurs of my soul
 call it the bursts of speed in my torso
  i don't need to speak
   there is a language in time
    it looks like little rainbow balls which stack up the emptiness
   between objects
    where the speed and colour take their course
    sink
      lucky ones find diamond events that are crystal clear
      and soon you'll go back to old habits
        this will go somewhere between a dream and a memory
       you will call blandness reality
      so here's a reminder
       the door is always open
         the price of entry is just a little release
        a pain the rises up from tight muscles

It's a fine line between inside and out
 someone opening a door draws a diagram
  with a rock of doom

Which way is that thing I don't like?

   or a warming chest
    there is a meniscus
     a passing through
      bubbles on their way

agave

Playlists are born
 because picking the next song is a little stressful
  but lord knows I don't want to listen to other people's music

I'm in a party mood
 and so are you
  you think that everything that you experience
   happens because of me
   would you be willing to entertain the possibility that I am
   not a warlock?
    maybe i just really turn you on

But that's ok
 because in other contexts
  i also viciously renounce agency
   and we're listening to your songs tonight
    the ones that remind you how sad you used to be

Which way is that thing I don't like?

listen to your body?

Things to continue with

The breath
 and words I spoke to myself
  when I once spoke kindly

And what were those things?
 here's something
  'don't judge your feelings
   they're just messengers'
   ok so
    what are they saying?
     the tight chest says
      have a cigarette
       and break up with your girlfriend
       seems a bit extreme

panic

Things spiral out of themselves
　make sense in little stitchings
　　but forget each other end to end
　　　there are pots with crusted oatmeal
　　　　plywood desks posturing as polished oak
　　　　　lukewarm tea and the distant bass thud
　　　　　　it's Saturday night the threads have fallen apart

Sour bubbles stomach to throat
　i'm panicking

So what's happening?
　i feel like doing something destructive
　　she says that's just trauma re-enactment
　　　it's better to sit still and see if you can cry

astro girl

She's doing research on my asteroid kinks
  it makes a lot of sense
    that i'm into Scorpios

It's unlikely that we will have sex
 until her Saturn return finishes
  her strange language
    the one where she sets her boundaries

I take a photo of the living room
 under the purple light
  the bed on the floor,
   and endless empty cups
     one day this photo will spell doom

And when she leaves
  i need to clean up
  buy some toilet paper
   try to do
     what i would otherwise be doing

whats the gasometer?

I'm eating an ice cream.
 you spontaneously say 'ketchup'
  you're thinking about pizza,
   that's cool
    keep thinking about it

rest

Having something to do
 makes me want to do nothing
  i flirt with a fantasy
   of undiagnosed ADHD
    and cheap dexamphetamine

Treasures come out of nowhere when you shake off to do lists
 and joy's aperture gets wider when you shake off contempt
  when you stop shooting your shame outward
   i've got a high horse,
    but Kylie Minogue isn't beneath me

Lying in bed on a sunny day
 it's a good thing to waste a day here and there

girlfriend

Ash on the bed
 this is the weirdest doob yet
  i channelled her broski ex
   food faced and saying half truths
    i think we're gonna go to Nicaragua
     we're not getting married
      although one day we might be de facto

She writes a lot, and so do i
 but never at the same time
  the pen is the power
   the other one stares and talks compulsively
   and tries to make their way onto the page

But I throw her things to read
 so i can focus on what i'm doing
  she likes the way i talk about myself
   stoic, exhausted, dissociated
    but fundamentally cool

Pissing with the door open
 being lazy like that
   you are my girlfriend
    after all

take some time

You're sad
 but the worst part is that you feel guilty about it
  take some time to feel and rest
   and later we'll talk about letting go of expectations
    of how you ought to feel

I go onto psychology forums and breathe a sigh of relief
 after i accumulate an impressive catalogue of diagnoses
  after Instagram and the twilight of subjectivity
   after we pray for disease
    after we realise that no matter how we contort our bodies
     this hard bed will never feel comfortable

You're sad
 take some time to feel and rest
  if not for yourself
   do it for the ones to come
    because you can either feel it through
     or you can pass it on
      either way, someone has to bleed.

trust

Take a ride on a burst of black speed
 an excuse to scratch
  and lose control at the door
   the trickster says it's ego
    wanting to stand out
     the things you learn at the door
      make you special wounded and deep
       the hurting one
        wearing a badge of honour
         the suffering club
          the ones where it wasn't their fault

Which way is that thing I don't like?

big wound

The fire gets bigger as it retreats
  there is a toll of bad feeling to exit numbness
    then i hope for immense gentleness, resist and accept
      the slow landing, finding growing patches of safety
        these scratches have festered for a long while
          they sting on contact with the air
            fighting myself every step of the way
              finding ways to forgive in the second motion
              a bleeding heart which hoarded its love
              finally rears it's catch

Completely directionless
 and that's just the feeling of unburdening
  take three anchors in the endless draft of air
   you are here
    you love yourself
     you are allowed to do nothing

Mantras are great when you're winning
 but when you're feeling shit
  you would rather fantasize about all the things around you
  you can blame
   or find your own bloodshot eyes in the mirror
    and say i love you over and over again
     all the while feeling like your inner demon
      is tricking you into having sex with yourself

continued

Everything was disconnected
 anxiety was shame and shame was pain
  pain was grief and grief is love

Not coping or soothing or wading
 and dodging through the phantom voices in your head
  not pleasing or avoiding
   keeping yourself unsafely locked away

Soon a straight back,
 light shoulders and directed gaze
  who are you other than a home for my care
   who am I but the person I choose to be

I hope when i wake up
 when i come down
  when i fall back into the flinching
   and the comfort of worrying
    i'll read some nice words
     and they will mean something

rest again

Heavy
 music
  I don't like it
   smoothies with a shot of coffee
    kill two birds with one stone

Happy with buying things
 tired bodies, love-walking
  planning things we'll never do
   doing things we never plan

Healthily resisting myself
  going to sleep early

Watching tv doesn't make you a pawn
 trauma compulsions make you a robot
  the only oppression is living for tomorrow
   or eating the time and lives of other people
    who stand on the earth and feel
     safe and slow and
      speed was always a delayed promise
       a pillar of clear quartz in the receding horizon
        the first move, two steps
         and only one at a time

Dying for the king before you touch the cool waters
 i'm sinking into hot sand
  half a leg down it gets cold
   all this time the prize was waiting
    just root and sink
     and feel the true cadence of inertia against our to-do lists
      the slowing impulse of the earth
       the sat fear which comes to ice

Boca Sea God

Sometimes I want to lyricise about the wind
 the sky, the water, Natural Beauty ™
  but it feels a bit tacky
   but is that just an unhealed urge
    to send me back to my head
     continue the war against presence
      doing the complicated thing
       not the hard thing

Palm trees shake in the wind
 sweat squeezes out of my skin
  keeping pace with the rising sun
   I've ordered eggs which will probably
    only make me sweat more
     was that something to hold onto?

One part of me wants to pray to the sea god
 the other part feels like i'm too white
  one part is hellbent on getting high
   one part is shame bound and wants nothing more
    than to stay in the wasteland because big energy feels scary
     but it feels good to talk to the sea god
      i always said i wanted to have a spiritual phase

Which way is that thing I don't like?

I think i'm becoming my own therapist

Lying on the beach
 the aching lightning of anger in my arms
  beneath the fight i find a little boy
   a hurting child and scrunching faces

I close my eyes and imagine him on a playground
  cheer him on and help him up the top of the slide
   and when the one comes with clenched fists and cruel lips
    I stand in front of him,
     scoop him up in my arms
      he cries and i kiss his forehead

We get into the car
 i tell him how brave he is as we drive to the shops
  for ice cream and burgers
   and when we get home i tuck him into bed
    i tell him i love him

In the night he screams
 i open the door and see a magpie hovering over the bed
  claws clamped around the bed
   he's trapped
    and so in brash act
     i spear tackle the magpie
      causing it to blush and fly out the window
       he cries and i hold him
        and tell him that everything will be alright
       you can trust me
        i got this

I ate eggs

On the verandah with the best eggs we ever made
 the secret is to dress the butter in garlic
  yet stress and resentment still
   make diadems with dinner on the bed
    and a broken tap

But good food is good food
 it makes the spider rest
  in the off center heart of its web
   my power drips away
    rests in that fantasy where i'm the person i wanna be
     where my early sun, my cool air, my true companionship
     and my clear schedule
      feels as good as it sounds

But let's leave behind the self attack
 good eggs remember that birthing is continuous
  power given away circles back
   reincarnation in the navel
    you can listen to it,
     try it, you've always got something in your stomach dummy

Yes, i ate eggs
 and among other stifled births
  something is always ready
   never mind the botched carries
    never mind the guilt, the lost time

Which way is that thing I don't like?

Little Donkey Boy

Straw hats and dusty tennis courts
 dirty fences and loose chickens
  donkey boy relishes a courtside view
   i've always lived in the city
    but sometime my phone doesn't work

If they crack cheap fusion
 what will happen to the chickens
  when life finally happens on two times speed
   when we all stop believing in words
    and numbers too
     and the only real thing
      are the implanted memories
       of fields which tend themselves
        and donkey boys, never traumatised

latex chief

My girlfriend is the latex chief
 yesterday she wore bike shorts
  which makes me think she means business
   but apparently that's just fashion in Europe

She worries i love her less when she's grumpy
but i still think she's cute
 i love her intensity
  it wears many faces

But i do think she's too quick to judge hippies
 but i do love the way she wakes up in a storm
  because street dogs which bark
   and fight all night
    belie the semblance
     of flowy pants and being in touch

Sometimes the latex chief wears a cute dress
 and cries to i need a hero
  waiting for her throat chakra focaccia
   i want to hold her and smile when she finds herself
    when she finds the safety uncanny
     her suspicion will be the death of her
      but i'll keep knocking at her door
       offering my cup of devotion

which way is that thing I don't like

I have a new right handed fountain pen
 which safely disables itself
  for my girlfriend's 10% hand
   i also have a long graveyard
    of pens which disappointed me in the past

And which way is that thing i don't like?
 to my right is her phone,
  the interminable competition for her attention
  to my left is a graveyard
   north seems ok
    supplements and sunscreen
    a canned mojito, tempted
    it'll only make me tired
     inside i'm a swamp of exhaustion
      and good intentions
       a lion, creative flare, destructive impulses
       a teacher, or maybe i should go to that rally

South a city sown with parks and tourists
 a mix in my mind where I keep a hit list
  the top candidate is of course myself
   but then again, i'm more a coward than a monster
    apt to follow her
     becoming a warrior of love and light
      slaying demons and trauma traps
      with a single afternoon of doodling

So which way is that thing i don't like?
 well either you repressed it

or perhaps you let it go
    and because you like hurting yourself
     you want to find it again
      just to think about it
       quietly letting it repopulate the entire surface of your mind
        under the pretext that you're just
         "figuring it out"

And there goes a truck, or a car
 or another aborted bike path extension
  new urbanism and stupid cities
   now that's a cause worth fighting for
    a suitable channel for your stuck feelings

Everytime I stop I start again

Come the next botched revolution
 the royalists must articulate their rights
  from self-help paperbacks,
   'boundaries and non-negotiables'

Every time I stop I start again
 with a dazzling mantra
  a hollow feeling
  a tired inquiry
   which goes in circles
    i'm trying figure out the difference
     between identifying with feelings in an unhealthy way
      and heeding their message

What's it called when you can't tell the difference between two things?
 and how is that different between having two words
  which apply to the same little haecceity?
   let's conclude that it's just energy
    and you don't have to know what it means
     though it would be helpful
      to decode a pre-existing presence
       and bathe in the bad faith of knowing what i am

But i get it;
 anger is boundaries crossed
  sadness the resultant wound
   grief the beauty of letting it go
    fear the threat of it coming back

But what's a black swirl?
 or a snake rolling from your right shoulder
  to a throbbing sense of the future in your left temple
   and if meaning is just an excuse to act
    does that mean i can put my frozen goods in the fridge
     let them thaw out and promise that i'll eat them soon
      and feel animals and colours and three kinds of pepper
     where i'm supposed to feel emotions?

you can do things that never happened

It's my first time at Wendy's
 i've started smoking again
  cops at the next table
   they know i smoke weed
    luckily i don't have any on me

I embraced stoner culture ironically
 but in truth, i never abandoned the possibility
  that smoking weed is cool
   my first capitulation was quitting soft drink
    convinced that it was social death
     i learned to hide my smoking too
      keeping it as a secret badge of honour, showing itself at 2 AM
       when i pull out a Q
        in a weedy backyard with some diffident strangers

So yeah, i write poems about weed
 but i have a personality too
  and that's why the cops are scared
   because maybe i have a bit too much
    or is that just my shame
     telling me to get smaller
      under the pretext that i'm too cool to be known

Which way is that thing I don't like?

i'm allowed to leave reality if i want to

What's a good song to think to?
 what's it like to make life changing decisions?
  what's the difference between that
   and having the courage to go after what you want?

And how do you engineer situations where you can't be seen?
 the ones where a mask comfortably fits

  So you managed to cut some cords
   found a new frontier
    where you raised the murmurs of desire
    from the mud and the shame
     resisted yourself in all the right ways
      choose the music where a throat opens;
       where once you were stoned and paralysed
       in bed with your melancholic indie pop
        now you're saying things
         that you never told anyone

I'm allowed to leave reality if i want to
 resentful fantasies, magnanimously humiliating people you love
 or simple scenarios where different rules apply
  staying up when everyone else has gone to bed
   taking revenge for all the time they took
    but now we unlock little vapours of hope;
     the other fantasy where magic is real
      with a body at rest

And of course, I'm allowed to leave reality if I want to
 trust me i will
  but what about sitting down for a few months

Which way is that thing I don't like?

   with books and pens and a clear schedule
    nothing but you and the old voices
     the ones which like to wear your face
      but listening to that other kind of music
       that speaks destiny against an offer to leave

About the Author

Nick is a writer and disability support worker. He lives on the land of the Wurundjeri Woi-wurrung and Bunurong peoples.

Email: *nickpcrowleywrite@gmail.com*

www.ingramcontent.com/pod-product-compliance
Lightning Source LLC
Chambersburg PA
CBHW022021290426
44109CB00015B/1268